Dinosaur World

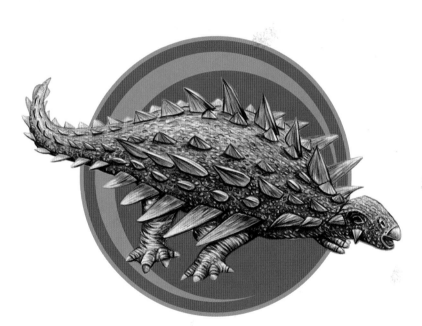

Bath · New York · Singapore · Hong Kong · Cologne · Delhi · Melbourne

Dinosaur World

Travel back in time to when dinosaurs
ruled our Earth

Photo credits: p28 centre Louis Psihoyos/Corbis; pp28-29 center
Paul A. Sanders/Corbis; p29 top Louis Psihoys/Corbis

Original text by John Malam and Steve Parker, adapted by
Jinny Johnson
Consultant: Dr John A. Cooper

First published by Parragon in 2008
Parragon
Queen Street House
4 Queen Street
Bath BA1 1HE, UK

ISBN 978-1-4075-4457-1
Printed in China

Contents

The world of the dinosaurs

No human being has ever seen a living, breathing dinosaur. But we still know a lot about these creatures that lived millions of years ago. Scientists can study fossilized bones and teeth. They compare them with those of living animals to figure out how dinosaurs looked and how they lived.

Earth's history

There were creatures living on land 150 million years before the dinosaurs, and the first tiny life forms lived in the ocean more than 2,000 million years ago.

Eras and periods

Earth's history is divided into lengths of time called eras. The dinosaurs lived in the Mesozoic era. Each era is split into smaller lengths of time called periods.

Cenozoic era (Recent life)	Quaternary period	Holocene Epoch (0.01–Now)* *Most of recorded history*
		Pleistocene Epoch (2–0.01) *Early humans spread*
	Tertiary Period (65–2) *Rise of mammals and birds*	
Mesozoic era (Middle life)	Cretaceous Period (144–65) *Last of the dinosaurs*	
	Jurassic Period (206–144) *Dinosaurs reach their greatest size*	
	Triassic Period (250–206) *Many reptiles, first dinosaurs*	
Paleozoic era (Ancient life)	Permian Period (286–250) *Mammal-like reptiles*	
	Carboniferous Period (360–286) *Many amphibians, first reptiles*	
	Devonian Period (408–360) *First amphibians walk on land*	
	Silurian Period (438–408) *Plants spread from water to land*	

All numbers are millions of years ago

How time is divided

The eras and periods are figured out according to the way the rocks of the time formed and the fossils in those rocks.

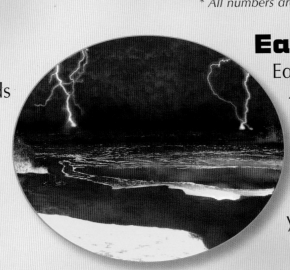

Early Earth

Earth was formed about 4,600 million years ago. At first nothing could live on Earth, but life began about 3,000 million years ago.

Moving continents

The world's land has slowly moved and split into the continents we know today.

In the Triassic, all the land was in one mass known as Pangaea.

The Triassic period

The earliest dinosaur fossils have been found in rocks dating from the middle of the Triassic period, about 230 million years ago.

Plant life

The most common trees in the Triassic were conifers, ginkgoes, and palmlike cycads. Smaller plants included ferns, mosses, and horsetails.

Did you know?

The world was so warm during the Triassic that there was no ice at the North and South Poles.

Triassic weather

The world's weather was very different in the Triassic. It was much warmer than it is now and there was less rain. This meant there were large areas of desert and dry scrubland.

There were huge
deserts in the
middle of the land.

Fewer trees could
grow in the dry
Triassic heat.

Triassic map

At this time, there was just one big
landmass we call Pangaea. All
around it was the Panthalassa
Ocean. But the Tethys Sea was
beginning to divide Pangaea in two.

Panthalassa

Pangaea

Tethys Sea

Small rivers flowed
during the rainy
season.

Triassic animals

There were many kinds
of reptiles as well as
dinosaurs in the Triassic.
These included mammal-
like reptiles, crocodiles,
and turtles. The first
mammals had also appeared.

The Jurassic period

At the start of the Jurassic period, about 200 million years ago, the world began to change again. The climate became cooler and more plants grew.

Huge swamps and bogs developed in low-lying areas.

Plant life

Plants began to grow in areas that had been deserts. The main trees were still conifers. Smaller plants included clubmosses, ferns, and horsetails.

Did you know?

The world's continents are still moving, but only at the rate of about an inch a year.

Jurassic weather

The weather was warmer than today, but not as hot as it had been during the Triassic. The climate was much the same all over the world, with long rainy seasons and short dry seasons.

More rain and less heat allowed large forests to grow.

Jurassic map
Pangaea separated into two large areas of land. These were Gondwana in the south and Laurasia in the north.

L A U R A S I A

Tethys Sea

G O N D W A N A

There were a lot of rivers and lakes and plenty of fish.

Jurassic animals
Dinosaurs became more and more common during the Jurassic and there were a lot of smaller reptiles, too, such as lizards. There were insects, snails, and spiders, and the first birds appeared.

The Cretaceous period

During the Cretaceous period the world became more like it is today. It started to be much colder at the Poles and hotter near the equator.

Moving continents caused many mountains to appear.

Plant life

Flowering plants, like those we know today, first appeared in this period. Trees, such as oak, magnolia, walnut, and maple, began to grow.

Did you know?

At least 1,000 different kinds of dinosaur have been discovered and there may be many more.

Cretaceous weather

The seasons became more varied at this time. In the north and south, there were winters and summers. Nearer the equator there were wet and dry seasons.

There was less rain so fewer trees could grow in the forests.

Cretaceous map

Laurasia and Gondwana broke up into the continents we know today. The Americas drifted away from Europe and Africa, so the Atlantic Ocean became wider.

North America

Europe

Asia

South America

Africa

India

Australia

Antarctica

Fish and shellfish thrived in the rivers and shallow seas.

Cretaceous animals

There were more kinds of dinosaur than ever, as well as other reptiles, such as snakes. Birds flew in the skies along with flying reptiles called pterosaurs. There were some small mammals.

15

Dinosaur skeletons

Most of what we know about dinosaurs comes from studying their fossilized bones and teeth.

Dinosaur posture

A dinosaur's legs were held straight down under its body. (The legs of reptiles, such as lizards, stick out to the sides of the body.)

Hip bones

Dinosaurs can be divided into two groups depending on the shape of their hip bones.

Pointing backward (Ornithischian)

Pointing forward (Saurischian)

Hip joint socket

Ilium

Ischium

Pubis

Pubis

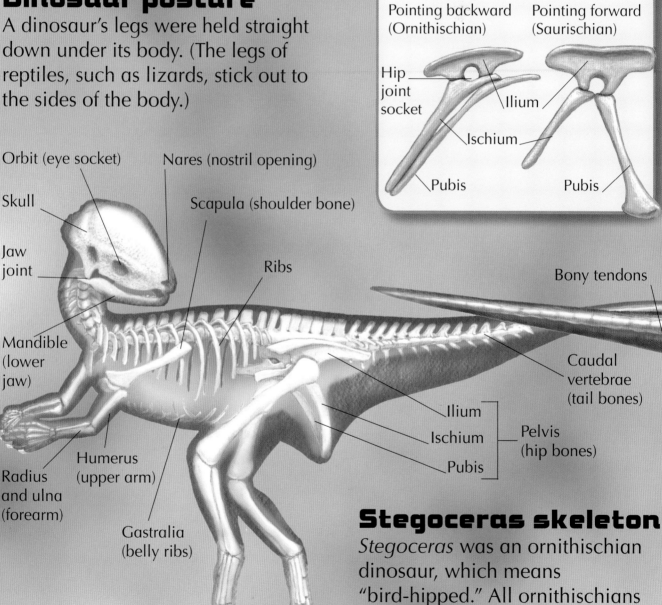

Orbit (eye socket)

Nares (nostril opening)

Skull

Scapula (shoulder bone)

Jaw joint

Ribs

Bony tendons

Mandible (lower jaw)

Caudal vertebrae (tail bones)

Ilium

Ischium

Pelvis (hip bones)

Pubis

Humerus (upper arm)

Radius and ulna (forearm)

Gastralia (belly ribs)

Stegoceras skeleton

Stegoceras was an ornithischian dinosaur, which means "bird-hipped." All ornithischians fed on plants.

Joint types

A tendon joins a muscle to a bone. Some dinosaurs had stiff bony tendons on their tail joints, making the tail extra strong and very rigid.

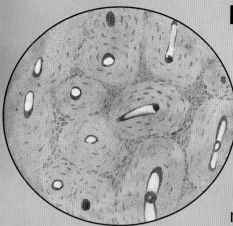

Inside bone

The bones of some fast-running dinosaurs, such as *Deinonychus,* show that they may have been warm-blooded like mammals, not cold-blooded like most reptiles.

Did you know?

More dinosaur fossils have been found in North America and Asia than anywhere else.

Deinonychus skeleton

Deinonychus was a saurischian dinosaur, which means "lizard-hipped." There were meat eaters and plant eaters in this group of dinosaurs.

Brain case

Cervical vertebrae (neck bones)

Sacral vertebrae (hip backbones)

Tibula and fibula (shin bones)

Knee joint

Femur (thigh bone)

Sickle claw on second toe

Phalanx (toe bone)

Ankle joint

Metatarsals (foot bones)

Dinosaur muscles and organs

Experts can figure out what dinosaur muscles and organs may have looked like by studying similar living animals.

Digestion

The big plant-eating dinosaurs swallowed their food whole. It was broken down inside the part of the body called the gizzard.

Brains

Models of a dinosaur's brain can be made using the shape of the space inside the skull.

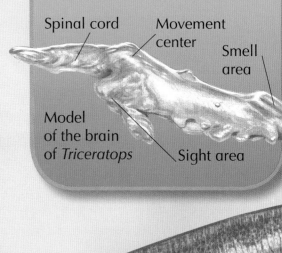

Spinal cord   Movement center   Smell area

Model of the brain of *Triceratops*   Sight area

Gizzard (muscular stomach)   Small intestine   Lung

Kidney

Reproductive opening

Secondary digestion chamber

Heart

Liver

Large intestine

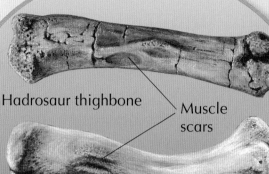

Hadrosaur thighbone

Muscle scars

Modern crocodile thighbone

Muscle scars

Experts check to see whether the marks of muscles on fossil dinosaur bones look like those on the bones of similar living animals. This helps them learn about the dinosaur.

Did you know? The first fossils of dinosaur footprints were found in the U.S. in 1802 by a young boy on a farm.

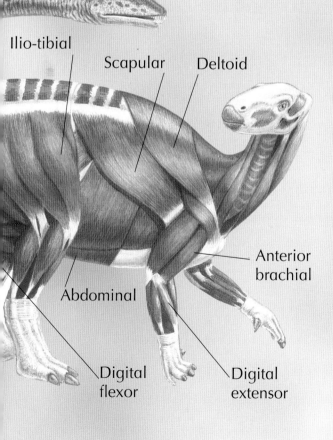

Ilio-tibial

Scapular   Deltoid

Abdominal

Anterior brachial

Digital flexor

Digital extensor

Clues to muscles

Marks on bones show where muscles were attached in life. This helps experts figure out how big the muscles might have been and how the animal moved.

Naming the muscles

Many muscles are named after their shape, such as the deltoid—deltoid means triangular. Others are named after the bones they are attached to such as the femoro-tibial (thigh-shin).

Death of the dinosaurs

From time to time a lot of living things become extinct, or die out completely. About 65 million years ago, dinosaurs and many other creatures disappeared from Earth.

Not only dinosaurs

Flying reptiles called pterosaurs in the air, and mosasaurs and plesiosaurs in the ocean also became extinct around 65 million years ago.

How long?

Dinosaurs were completely wiped out 65 million years ago. But 70 million years ago, there were already fewer dinosaurs than before.

The asteroid impact

An asteroid is a piece of rock from space. Some people think that an asteroid hit the Earth 65 million years ago, killing all the dinosaurs.

1. Asteroid hits Earth

2. Impact of the explosion spreads quickly

3. Dust and debris cause climate change

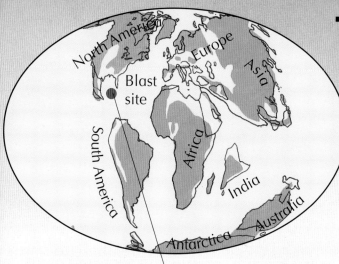

North America
Europe
Asia
Blast site
South America
Africa
India
Antarctica
Australia

An enormous crater found off the coast of Mexico may have been the asteroid's impact site.

The asteroid idea

If an asteroid did hit Earth 65 million years ago, it would have caused huge clouds of dust and debris to spread. This would have blocked out the sun for years, killing the plant life. Without plants, plant-eating animals died too, and then meat-eating animals.

Did you know?

The asteroid of 65 million years ago might have measured 6 miles across and traveled at 34 miles per second.

Death of the dinosaurs

There are a lot of other ideas about why the dinosaurs and other animals died out. Here are a few of these ideas.

Diseases

Perhaps dinosaurs and other animals were killed by a deadly disease that spread across the world.

Invisible rays from deep space

If a huge star had exploded in space, the radiation could have reached Earth. This would have killed large animals, such as dinosaurs. They could not hide underground like mammals.

Climate change

The movement of the world's land may have caused climate change. If the weather became very cold, dinosaurs might have frozen to death.

Choked to death

A lot of volcanoes were erupting 65 million years ago. The air might have been full of deadly poisonous smoke and dust.

No one reason

Perhaps there was no one thing that wiped out the dinosaurs. It could be that colder weather and volcanic explosions had already killed some. Finally, an asteroid wiped out the remaining dinosaurs.

The survivors

These ideas may explain why some animals were wiped out, but not why others lived. For example, if dinosaurs were killed by a disease, why did shellfish and some plants disappear, too?

How fossils are formed

Fossils are the remains of dead animals or plants. These became trapped in the ground and turned into rock over millions of years.

Heterodontosaurus skull

What forms fossils?

Usually only the hard parts of an animal are fossilized. So there are fossil bones, teeth, claws, and shells. There are many fossils of shelled ocean creatures, such as ammonites.

Teeth and bone fossils

As the tooth or bone lies in the ground, substances called minerals gradually sink into it. The tooth or bone stays the same shape but slowly turns to rock.

Ammonite

Tyrannosaurus tooth

Tyrannosaurus upper leg bone

Did you know? The oldest fossils of animals that have ever been found date from about 600 million years ago.

24

Bone to stone

The dead bodies of most animals rot away. Very few become fossils. But if the conditions are just right this is what happens over millions of years.

A dead dinosaur is washed into a river.

Over the years the bones are covered with layers of sand and earth, which becomes rock.

Minerals sink into the bone and change it to stone.

As the surface rock is worn away the fossils come to the surface.

Trace fossils

The shape of a footprint or a nest can also be turned to stone. This is called a trace fossil. Even droppings (coprolites) and egg shells can be fossilized.

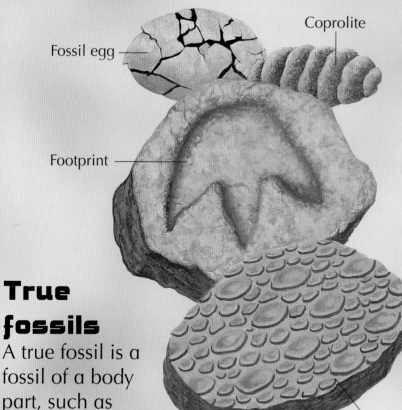

Fossil egg

Coprolite

Footprint

Fossil skin

True fossils

A true fossil is a fossil of a body part, such as bone or tooth. Some fossils of dinosaur skin have been found but these are very rare.

Perfectly preserved

Amber is formed from a sticky fluid called resin which oozes from a tree trunk. Some ancient pieces have been found with the remains of an insect trapped inside.

Digging for dinosaurs

Fossils are hard to find. But in some places, rocks from the age of the dinosaurs have been worn away by wind and weather so fossils are nearer the surface.

Searching for sites

Digging for fossils is hard work. Experts look for clues, such as a bone or tooth sticking out of a cliff or rock, to see if a dig may be worthwhile.

Every find is carefully labeled.

Tools and techniques

Explosives may be used to uncover fossils. Then a lot of tools, such as hammers and chisels, are used to break away the rock around the fossil.

The finds continue...

Dinosaur experts such as Paul Sereno are still finding new kinds of dinosaurs. Who knows what amazing creatures are still to be discovered?

Diggers must be careful not to damage fossils.

Did you know?

Dinosaur fossils have now been found in every continent of the world, even in Antarctica.

Displaying dinosaurs

You can see dinosaur fossils in museums in many countries of the world. Some museums also have lifelike models that move and even roar!

Cleaning

Tiny hand tools and brushes are used to take away every speck of dirt from a dinosaur fossil. The cleaning process can take weeks or even months.

Life-size dinosaurs are an amazing sight.

Preparing and sorting

Rebuilding a dinosaur from pieces of fossil is like a very difficult jigsaw puzzle. Experts use their knowledge of similar creatures to put the pieces together.

The right pose

Dinosaur experts do their best to display dinosaurs as they would have looked when they were alive.

Copied parts

It is very rare to find a whole dinosaur skeleton. So some parts have to be made to fill in the gaps. Sometimes the fossils are copied in light material, such as fiberglass.

Seeing inside rocks and fossils

Medical scanners are used to see inside fossils. They show what condition the fossil is in and whether it is worth cleaning and preparing.

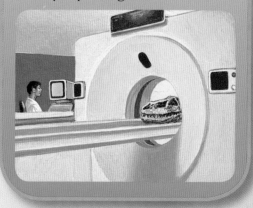

On display

At last, when everything has been put together and missing pieces filled in, the dinosaur goes on display. We can all admire a creature that lived so many millions of years ago.

Quick Quiz

Find the correct stickers to answer the questions below.

When did the dinosaurs die out?

Answer

6 years ago   650 years ago   65 million years ago

What are fossils made of?

Answer

rock   wood   leaves

Which of these dinosaurs might have been warm-blooded?

Answer

Deinonychus   Stegosaurus   Triceratops

Meat eaters

The first meat-eating dinosaurs appeared about 225 million years ago. They included the world's biggest-ever predators. These killers terrorized the world's plant eaters for more than 160 million years, until all the dinosaurs died out 65 million years ago.

Theropods

All meat-eating dinosaurs are called theropods. The name means "beast feet." Most of these dinosaurs moved upright on their slender back legs. They could run much faster than the plant eaters they hunted.

Creature features

Most of the meat-eating dinosaurs had birdlike feet with clawed toes. They had sharp-clawed hands for attacking and holding onto their prey.

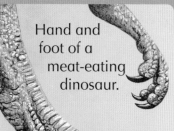

Hand and foot of a meat-eating dinosaur.

Daspletosaurus

Albertosaurus

Dromaeosaurus

Changes over time

Meat-eating dinosaurs adapted over millions of years. Later species were more intelligent and had longer legs and sharper eyes than earlier predators.

Dromiceiomimus

Troodon

Tyrannosaurus

Dromiceiomimus

Teeth and beaks

Many of the plant eaters had strong jaws and big teeth. Others had toothless beaks that might have been used for cracking eggs.

The first plant eaters

These dinosaurs first appeared about 225 million years ago, during the Triassic period. They were smaller than later predators, such as *Tyrannosaurus*, and not such fierce hunters.

Coelophysis

This dinosaur was built for speed. Its leg bones were almost hollow which made it light and able to run fast.

Coelophysis facts

Lived: 220 million years ago

Found: North America

Length: 10 feet

Eoraptor

One of the earliest dinosaurs, *Eoraptor* moved quickly on its slender back legs. It was a plant eater, but it may have also eaten animals that were already dead. This is called scavenging.

Eoraptor's long jaws were lined with a lot of small saw-edged teeth.

Eoraptor facts

Lived: 225 million years ago

Found: South America

Length: 3 feet

Herrerasaurus

Another fast-moving hunter, *Herrerasaurus* had arms that were much shorter than its legs. It held its tail straight out behind it when it ran to balance its weight.

Herrerasaurus facts

Lived: 220 million years ago

Found: South America

Length: 10 feet

Fast movers

Meat eaters had to be sure-footed as well as fast, so that when chasing prey they could turn quickly and still keep their balance.

Going fishing

Some of the small predators, such as *Eoraptor*, may have fed on fish as well as hunted land animals.

Large theropods

Later species of meat-eating dinosaurs were much bigger than the earliest types. These huge creatures had strong teeth for biting meat and sharp claws for tearing at their prey's skin.

Dilophosaurus

This dinosaur probably moved in groups, searching for prey. The crest on its head may have been brightly colored and used to attract mates or to communicate with others in its group.

Allosaurus

The largest meat eater of its time, *Allosaurus* was a huge creature with big powerful back legs and a thick S-shaped neck. Its teeth had jagged edges for slicing through flesh.

Dilophosaurus facts	
Lived: 190 million years ago	
Found: North America	
Length: 20 feet	

Scavengers

Meat-eating dinosaurs may have been scavengers as well as hunters. This means that they ate animals that had died of old age, or had been killed by others. By scavenging, an animal gets a meal without much effort.

Allosaurus facts

Lived: 140 million years ago

Found: North America

Length: 39 feet

Giganotosaurus

This massive hunter was even larger than *Tyrannosaurus*. Its biggest teeth were an amazing 8 inches long and could slice deep into the flesh of its prey.

Giganotosaurus facts

Lived: 90 million years ago

Found: South America

Length: 49 feet

Tyrannosaurus rex

One of the best known of all dinosaurs, this mighty hunter lived toward the end of the dinosaurs' rule on Earth.

Powerful killer

Tyrannosaurus was strongly built and walked upright on its two big back legs. It held its tail out behind it to help balance the weight of its heavy head and chest. It had good eyesight for spotting its prey at a distance.

Surprise attacker

Tyrannosaurus lived in open woodland and often sneaked up on plant-eating dinosaurs as they stood feeding peacefully. It got as close as it could before making a final high-speed dash and pouncing on its prey.

Big head

Tyrannosaurus had a huge head, up to 5 feet long. Its jaws were packed with 50 or 60 razor-sharp teeth. Some were 9 inches long.

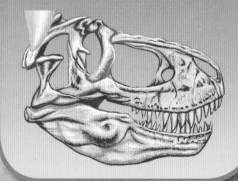

Full to bursting

Like lions and tigers today, *Tyrannosaurus* probably didn't eat every day. If it killed a large plant eater, it would gobble up as much as it could and be satisfied for several days.

Tyrannosaurus bursts out from the trees to attack a group of *Edmontosaurus* dinosaurs.

Small arms

This dinosaur's arms were so tiny they didn't even reach up to its mouth. But its claws were very useful for seizing hold of prey.

Tyrannosaurus facts

Lived: 70 million years ago

Found: North America

Length: 39 feet

Dromaeosaurs

All these dinosaurs were very fierce hunters. They had big sharp claws on their feet and strong hands for grabbing their prey.

Utahraptor

The claw on *Utahraptor*'s second toe was 15 inches long. The dinosaur attacked prey with these killer claws while holding on tight with its strong hands.

Utahraptor facts

Lived: 125 million years ago

Found: North America

Length: 21 feet

Dromaeosaurus

This dinosaur, like other dromaeosaurs, could speed along at almost 40 miles per hour. It had lots of sharp teeth and a large curved claw on each foot.

Dromaeosaurus facts

Lived: 70 million years ago

Found: North America

Length: 6 feet

Clever hunters

Dromaeosaurs probably hunted in packs, working together to bring down much larger animals.

Fossils have been found of *Velociraptor* attacking a *Protoceratops* dinosaur.

Velociraptor

Velociraptor had sharp, serrated teeth and a large hook-shaped claw on each foot. It held its claws off the ground when it wasn't attacking prey, so they wouldn't get worn down and dull.

Velociraptor facts	
Lived: 70 million years ago	
Found: Asia	
Length: 6 feet	

Quick Quiz

Find the correct stickers to answer the questions below.

Which of these dinosaurs had a head up to 5 feet long?

Answer

Tyrannosaurus rex

Troodon

Daspletosaurus

Which of these dinosaurs was the largest meat eater of its time?

Answer

Allosaurus

Dilophosaurus

Gigantosaurus

Which of these dinosaurs had a large hook-shaped claw on each foot?

Answer

Dromaeosaurus

Utahraptor

Velociraptor

Large plant eaters

Sauropods were the biggest of all the plant-eating dinosaurs. Experts think these huge long-necked dinosaurs were the largest animals that have ever lived on land.

Cetiosaurs

These were some of the earliest sauropods. All had a heavy body and a solid backbone. Some later sauropods had bones that were partly hollow, which made them lighter.

Cetiosaurus

Cetiosaurus is famous for being the first sauropod to be discovered. Its giant bones were found in England in 1809.

Barapasaurus

Barapasaurus had a long tail and neck like other cetiosaurs. Its spoon-shaped teeth had jagged edges for stripping leaves from branches.

Barapasaurus facts

Lived: 200 million years ago

Found: Asia

Length: 59 feet

Cetiosaurus facts

Lived: 175 million years ago

Found: Europe, Africa

Length: 59 feet

Shunosaurus facts

Lived: 170 million years ago

Found: China

Length: 33 feet

Shunosaurus

This cetiosaur had a spiky lump of bone at the end of its tail. It could use this to defend itself against attackers.

Camarasaurs

These sauropods first lived in the late Jurassic period. Unlike other giant plant eaters, camarasaurs had teeth that pointed forward.

Twigs

Camarasaurus was able to feed on the hard parts of plants because of its strong teeth.

Camarasaurus's teeth were more than 1½ inches wide.

Camarasaurus

This dinosaur's strong jaws were packed with big spoon-shaped teeth. They were shaped for cutting through twigs and branches.

Camarasaurus facts

Lived: 150 million years ago	
Found: N. America, Europe	
Length: 59 feet	

Euhelopus

Many sauropods had teeth only at the front of their mouth. *Euhelopus* had teeth all around its jaws, as did *Camarasaurus*.

Did you know?

Euhelopus's neck was an amazing 16 feet long and was made up of nine vertebrae. Even a giraffe has only seven vertebrae in its neck.

Camarasaurus skull

Its skull shows this dinosaur had big eyes and nostrils. It probably had good senses of sight and smell.

Nostril

Eye socket

Holes for muscles

Brachiosaurus

Huge *Brachiosaurus* had an amazingly long neck. This meant it could reach out and munch a lot of different plants without moving far.

A good sense of smell

Brachiosaurus had big nostrils at the top of its head. It may have had a good sense of smell, so it could smell food and other animals before it could see them.

Nostril

Eye socket

Brachiosaurus dinosaurs would have stripped the leaves from trees.

Miniature brain

This huge creature had a small head and a tiny brain for its body. Its front legs were longer than its back legs, so its body sloped down toward its short tail.

Living in a group

Brachiosaurus probably moved around in a herd, or group. The dinosaurs would have spent most of their time looking for food and eating.

Did you know?

A big animal such as *Brachiosaurus,* needed a lot of food. It may have eaten 90 pounds of plants every day.

High and low

Brachiosaurus may have reared up on its back legs to reach high leaves. Or it may have kept all four feet firmly on the ground as it swung its long neck from side to side to find food.

Brachiosaurus facts

Lived: 150 million years ago

Found: Africa, Europe, N. America

Length: 82 feet

Diplodocus

This is one of the biggest and best known of the diplodocids. Experts used to think it dragged its tail on the ground. But fossilized tracks show that it held its tail up as it walked.

Fern-eater

Diplodocus probably couldn't lift its head very high. So it may have eaten lots of low-growing plants, such as ferns.

10-ton beast

Although *Diplodocus* was very long, it weighed only 10 tons. This was less than some other sauropods. The dinosaur was light for its size because many of the bones in its back were hollow.

Extra bones

There was an extra bone beneath each of the vertebrae making up this dinosaur's backbone. These extra bones strengthened the tail.

50

Long neck, tiny head

This giant dinosaur's neck grew up to about 26 feet long. But its head was tiny. It measured only about 20 inches.

Teeth

Diplodocus teeth

Diplodocus had 50–60 weak teeth in the front of its mouth, but no teeth for chewing food.

Diplodocus facts

Lived: 150 million years ago

Found: North America

Length: 88 feet

Titanosaurs

This group of sauropods first lived in the late Jurassic period. Their name means "gigantic lizards."

Argentinosaurus facts

Lived: 90 million years ago

Found: South America

Length: 98 feet

Alamosaurus

So far, *Alamosaurus* is the only titanosaur from North America. It lived until the end of the Cretaceous period, 65 million years ago, when dinosaurs were wiped out.

Alamosaurus facts

Lived: 70 million years ago

Found: North America

Length: 69 feet

Argentinosaurus

This enormous creature may have weighed as much as 100 tons. Only the biggest meat eaters, such as *Giganotosaurus*, would have dared to attack such a monster.

Body armor

Saltasaurus's skin was studded with many pieces of bone. These helped protect it from meat eaters' sharp teeth and claws.

Saltasaurus

Saltasaurus had a long neck and tail like other sauropods. But it also had special bony plates on its skin that may have acted like a suit of armor.

Saltasaurus facts

Lived: 80 million years ago	
Found: South America	
Length: 39 feet	

Quick Quiz

Find the correct stickers to answer the questions below.

Which of these dinosaurs was the first cetiosaur to be discovered?

Cetiosaurus

Barapasaurus

Shunosaurus

Answer

Which of these dinosaurs had an amazingly long neck?

Answer

Brachiosaurus

Camarasaurus

Euhelopus

Which of these dinosaurs had armored skin?

Alamosaurus

Argentinosaurus

Saltasaurus

Answer

54

Armored dinosaurs

Sauropods were not the only plant-eating dinosaurs. Other kinds included armored dinosaurs, stegosaurs, and horned dinosaurs. They were all smaller than sauropods, and they had their own built-in body armor.

Stegosaurus

Stegosaurus was the biggest stegosaur. A lot of fossils have been found, so it is also the best known of its family.

Roof reptile

When fossils of this dinosaur were first found, experts thought that the bony plates laid flat, covering the animal's back like a turtle's shell. Because of this, the dinosaur was given the name *Stegosaurus*, which means "roofed reptile." Later, they realized that the plates actually stood upright.

Did you know? The skin covering the plates on a stegosaur's back may have flushed red with blood when the animal was excited or scared.

Spiky tail

Stegosaurus was a slow-moving plant eater. It probably moved around in small groups. If attacked, *Stegosaurus* could not run away quickly, so it stood still, and defended itself against its enemy with its spiky tail.

Stegosaurus plate pattern

Experts aren't sure how the bony plates were arranged. They may have been in one row, in pairs or overlapping in a staggered row.

Two males fight over a female *Stegosaurus*. They turn their bodies sideways to show off their full size.

Stegosaurus facts

Lived: 140 million years ago

Found: North America

Length: 30 feet

57

The nodosaurs

The first armored dinosaurs were the nodosaurs. They all had lumps of bone set into the skin on their backs. This made them much harder for meat-eating dinosaurs to attack.

Minmi

Minmi even had large pieces of bone protecting its soft belly, as well as studs and spikes on its back.

Bony plates covered *Minmi*'s belly.

Gastonia

This dinosaur was a scary sight. It had big sharp spikes sticking out of its sides as well as bony studs on its back.

Gastonia facts

Lived: 125 million years ago

Found: North America

Length: 8 feet

The spikes were up to 1 foot long.

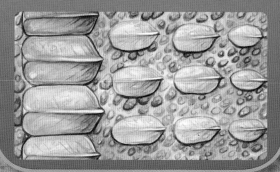
Body armor

The skin of armored dinosaurs was covered with pieces of bone. Some were flat, others pointed. In between were little bony lumps, about the size of a pea.

Edmontonia

Huge spines grew from the shoulders and sides of this dinosaur. They faced forward and probably protected it from predators.

Ankylosaurus

This dinosaur was one of the largest ankylosaurs. It had a big rounded body, shaped like a barrel, and was twice as wide as it was tall. Its legs were short but strong.

Body armor

The top of *Ankylosaurus*'s body was covered with thick plates of bone. Rows of big sharp spikes grew along the dinosaur's back, and it had horns at the back of its head. Only its belly was unprotected.

Ankylosaurus skull

At the front of *Ankylosaurus*'s jaws was a wide, toothless beak. Farther back were a lot of small teeth which it used for chewing food.

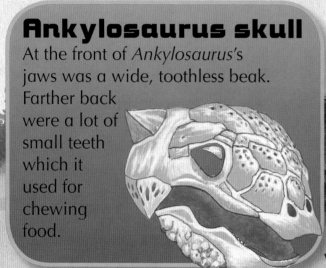

Ankylosaurus facts

Lived: 70 million years ago

Found: North America

Length: 33 feet

Warning sign

If attacked, *Ankylosaurus* would defend itself with its clubbed tail. Its skin may have blushed red as a warning sign that the dinosaur was getting angry.

Low feeder

Ankylosaurus had short legs and couldn't reach up to high branches. It fed on low-growing plants, which it snapped up with its wide beak.

A tyrannosaur is wounded by a blow from *Ankylosaurus*'s clubbed tail.

Ankylosaurus tail club

The heavy club at the end of *Ankylosaurus*'s tail was made of two balls of bones joined together.

Pachycephalosaurs

These creatures are often called bone-heads or bone-headed dinosaurs. This is because they had a thick lump of bone on the head.

Stygimoloch had lots of lumps and bumps on its head.

Speedy

Pachycephalosaurs were probably fast movers. They stood upright and raced around on their long back legs.

Stygimoloch

This is the only pachycephalosaur that had spikes on its head. These measured up to 6 inches long. Experts thin that maybe only male *Stygimoloch* dinosaurs had spikes.

Stygimoloch facts	
Lived: 70 million years ago	
Found: North America	
Length: 10 feet	

Prenocephale

Prenocephale may have had a big head, but there was only a tiny brain inside. The bony dome was ringed with little spikes and lumps of bone.

Stones

Pachycephalosaurs probably swallowed stones to help crush food in the stomach.

Pachycephalosaurus

This dinosaur was the largest of the bone-heads. The bony dome on top of its had was an amazing 10 inches thick.

Triceratops

Triceratops is the most famous of the ceratopsians, or horned dinosaurs. It had three sharp horns on its head, and its name means "three-horned face."

Strong body

Triceratops had a big chunky body, short tail, and thick legs. It weighed about 10 tons and was strong enough to fight off even fierce hunters, such as tyrannosaurs.

Triceratops skull

This dinosaur's neck frill was made of solid bone. The horns on top of its head were up to 3 feet long, but the nose horn was smaller.

Frill

Horn

Hole for eye

Nose horn

Nostril

Some adult *Triceratops* fight off a tyrannosaur.

Triceratops facts

Lived: 70 million years ago	
Found: North America	
Length: 30 feet	

Protecting the weak

Triceratops lived in a herd, or group, of animals. Young animals stayed in the center of the group, where they were safe from attackers.

Plant eater

Triceratops looks very fierce, but like other ceratopsians, it only ate plants. It bit off mouthfuls of leaves with its sharp beak.

Big battles

Triceratops probably fought over mates or who would lead the herd. They crashed their heads together and locked horns.

65

Quick Quiz

Find the correct stickers to answer the questions below.

Which of these dinosaurs had big plates on its back?

Answer

Gastonia

Stegosaurus

Edmontonia

Which of these dinosaurs had a clubbed tail?

Answer

Ankylosaurus

Minmi

Stegosaurus

Which of these dinosaurs had spikes on its head up to 6 inches long?

Answer

Stygimoloch

Prenocephale

Pachycephalosaurus

"Bird-feet" dinosaurs

Many new kinds of plant-eating dinosaurs, such as duckbills and iguanodonts, appeared in the Jurassic and Cretaceous periods. All had a bony beak for biting into plants and strong teeth for chewing.

Ornithopods

These dinosaurs are called "bird-feet" dinosaurs because they walked upright and on tip-toe like birds. There were a lot of different kinds of ornithopods living all over the world.

"Different-teeth" dinosaurs

These dinosaurs were also called heterodontosaurs. They had three kinds of teeth shaped for cutting, chewing, and stabbing.

Did you know?

Many ornithopods lived in big groups, called herds, made up of thousands of animals.

Parksosaurus

Different sizes

The smallest ornithopods were only about 6½ feet long. The biggest were over 60 feet long.

Iguanodon 33 feet long

Hypsilophodon
8 feet long

"High-ridge-teeth" dinosaurs

These dinosaurs were also called hypsilophodonts. *Parksosaurus* was an hypsilophodont.

Duckbills

These dinosaurs are known as duckbills because of their beaks, which looked like a duck's beak. They are also called hadrosaurs, which means "big lizards." *Edmontosaurus* and *Parasaurolophus* were duckbills.

Beaks

Ornithopod dinosaurs had bony beaks at the front of their jaws. These were covered with a hard material called horn. Their beaks were just right for biting off mouthfuls of plants.

Edmontosaurus

Hypsilophodon

Edmontosaurus

Parasaurolophus

Iguanodonts

The name of this group of dinosaurs means "iguana teeth." They got this name because people thought their teeth looked like those of iguana lizards. *Iguanodon* is the best known iguanodont.

Heterodontosaurs

These dinosaurs were the first of the ornithopods. They appeared about 220 million years ago and were all small plant eaters that walked upright on two legs.

Types of teeth

At the front of the mouth, behind the beak, were small, sharp teeth for biting. Then came two pairs of tusklike teeth. At the back of the mouth were a lot of wider teeth for chewing food.

The strong tail was held straight out and off the ground.

Heterodontosaurus

Like most heterodontosaurs, this dinosaur had short arms and long, slender back legs. It was probably a fast runner. Possibly only males had the big tusklike teeth.

Heterodontosaurus facts

Lived: 205 million years ago

Found: South Africa

Length: 4 feet

Abrictosaurus

This dinosaur did not have long tusklike teeth. It may have been a female *Heterodontosaurus* and not a separate species.

Cheek pouches

As a heterodontosaur chewed, the food collected in its fleshy cheek pouches. The dinosaur then used its tongue to move the food back to its jaws.

Pisanosaurus

Pisanosaurus was one of the first heterodontosaurs and one of the earliest dinosaurs. Only some of its bones have been found, not a whole skeleton.

Hypsilophodonts

These dinosaurs lived like antelopes and deer do today. They moved around in herds, feeding on low-growing plants.

Hypsilophodon

Hypsilophodon ate plants, such as ferns and horsetails. It had a lot of ridged teeth for chewing its food.

Built for speed

Hypsilophodonts were fast movers, too. They could probably run at up to 25 miles per hour for a short time.

Horsetails

Dinosaurs ate these plants. They first grew more than 400 million years ago and still grow today.

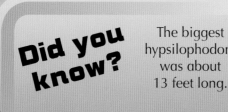

Did you know? The biggest hypsilophodont was about 13 feet long.

Hypsilophodon facts

Lived: 120 million years ago

Found: Europe, N. America

Length: 8 feet

Fulgurotherium facts

Lived: 130 million years ago

Found: Australia

Length: 6½ feet

Fulgurotherium

This dinosaur lived very far south. It may have moved north in winter to escape the icy weather.

Thescelosaurus

This was one of the last of the hypsilophodonts. It lived right at the end of the Age of Reptiles.

Thescelosaurus facts

Lived: 70 million years ago

Found: North America

Length: 13 feet

Iguanodon

This dinosaur was called *Iguanodon*, which means "iguana teeth," because the people who named it thought that its teeth looked like those of the iguana lizard.

Horse head

Iguanodon was a big animal with a long, stiff tail. It had a long head like a horse and its jaws were filled with a lot of sharp teeth.

Two legs or four

This dinosaur could walk upright on its two back legs or on all fours. It could run at speeds of up to 12 miles per hour.

Spiked thumb

Iguanodon had four clawed fingers and a big spiky thumb. It could bend its little finger across its hand to help it hold onto things, such as twigs and leaves.

Ground to a pulp

Using the strong beak at the front of its mouth, *Iguanodon* bit off leaves and twigs to eat. It chewed its food for a long time until it was just a mushy pulp.

Using the thumb

Iguanodon could have used its thumb spike like a knife to defend itself from meat-eating dinosaurs.

Iguanodon facts

Lived: 130 million years ago

Found: Asia, Europe, N. America

Length: 33 feet

Hadrosaurs

These dinosaurs are also called "duckbills" because they have a beak like a duck's. They were one of the last types of dinosaur and lived until the end of the Age of Reptiles.

Saurolophus

This hadrosaur had a long bony spike on the back of its head. This may have been covered with a flap of skin, making a bag that made the dinosaur's honking calls louder.

Hadrosaurus

A skeleton of this dinosaur was found in the U.S. in 1857. It was the first nearly complete dinosaur skeleton ever found.

Hadrosaurus facts

Lived: 75 million years ago	
Found: North America	
Length: 30 feet	

Ducklike mouths

It's easy to see why these dinosaurs are called duckbills. The beak at the front of the mouth was wide and flat. It was covered with a hard material called horn.

Saurolophus facts

Lived: 70 million years ago

Found: Asia, North America

Length: 39 feet

Lambeosaurus

Both male and female *Lambeosaurus* had bony crests on their heads. The males also had a spike of solid bone behind the crest.

The head crest may have made the dinosaur's calls louder.

Lambeosaurus facts

Lived: 70 million years ago

Found: North America

Length: 30 feet

Quick Quiz

Find the correct stickers to answer the questions below.

Which of these dinosaurs lived very far south?

Answer

Hypsilophodon   Thescelosaurus   Fulgurotherium

Which of these dinosaurs had a spiked thumb?

Answer

Iguanodon   Abrictosaurus   Heterodontosaurus

The first nearly complete dinosaur skeleton ever discovered was of...?

Answer

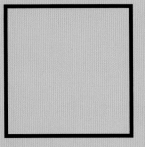

Hadrosaurus   Lambeosaurus   Saurolophus

The teeming oceans

No dinosaurs lived in the ocean, although some of them may have been able to splash their way across a lake or river. But the oceans were full of other creatures, such as fish and shellfish. There were also several kinds of large ocean-living reptiles, including plesiosaurs, pliosaurs, and ichthyosaurs.

The ancient oceans

Large, swimming reptiles ruled the oceans during the age of the dinosaurs. All were hunters, and ate fish and other ocean creatures.

Taking a breath
Ocean-living reptiles did not have gills like fish. So they had to come to the surface regularly to breathe.

Other ocean creatures
All these creatures lived alongside the ocean-living reptiles. Ammonites were very common then but are now extinct.

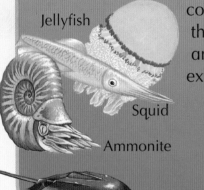

Jellyfish

Squid

Ammonite

Horseshoe crab

Turtle

Archelon

Ichthyosaur

Ocean reptiles
Ichthyosaurs, pliosaurs, and plesiosaurs became extinct at the same time as the dinosaurs. They died out forever. But other reptiles, such as turtles, still live in our oceans.

Seafood

There had been fish living in the ocean for 300 million years before the dinosaurs appeared. Sharks had already been the top predators in the ocean for 200 million years.

Plesiosaur

Pliosaur

Flippers to paddle

These swimming reptiles had bodies shaped to speed quickly through the water. And they had flippers instead of legs.

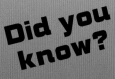

Did you know? Ichthyosaurs probably gave birth to live young in the water instead of laying eggs like land reptiles.

Plesiosaurs

These ocean-living reptiles first lived about 200 million years ago. They had small heads and long necks. They fed mostly on fish and other small ocean creatures.

Plesiosaurus

This was one of the first plesiosaurs. Like other plesiosaurs, it probably "flew" through the water by flapping its long flippers up and down, like turtles do today.

Plesiosaurus facts

Lived: 200 million years ago

Found: Europe

Length: 8 feet

Cryptoclidus facts

Lived: 150 million years ago

Found: Europe

Length: 12 feet

Cryptoclidus

Cryptoclidus had many smaller joints in its flippers. This gave the flipper a smoother and more flexible curved surface.

Long curved
flippers for
swimming
power

Caught in a cage

A plesiosaur's toothy jaws made a trap for prey. When the reptile opened its mouth, water and fish flowed in. When it closed its mouth, the fish were trapped inside.

Muraenosaurus

Half the length of this huge creature was its neck, and its head was very tiny. It probably swung its neck back and forth as it snapped up mouthfuls of food.

Muraenosaurus facts

Lived: 150 million years ago

Found: Europe

Length: 20 feet

Elasmosaurus

Elasmosaurus was the longest of the plesiosaurs and more than half its length was made up of its huge neck. It was also one of the last of the plesiosaurs.

More bones

Most reptiles have between five and ten vertebrae in their neck. But *Elasmosaurus* had more than 70, making its long neck very bendy.

Eyes on top

Elasmosaurus's eyes were on top of its head. It could see fish swimming above it and reach up to catch them.

Plesiosaur skull

Elasmosaurus had a long, low head. Its pointed nose helped it cut through the water and its long teeth made a perfect trap for fish.

The long neck could be twisted and turned very quickly.

Could they survive?

Scientists think that plesiosaurs died out with the dinosaurs 65 million years ago. But some people believe they may still be living in deep lakes today.

Elasmosaurus held its long neck straight out in front of its body.

Fast predator

Elasmosaurus probably ate small prey, such as fish, squid, and ammonites. It could move its long neck very swiftly to reach and catch its prey.

Did you know?

Elasmosaurus's huge neck measured an amazing 26 feet. That's as long as four tall men lying in a line.

Elasmosaurus facts

Lived: 70 million years ago	
Found: Asia, North America	
Length: 46 feet	

Pliosaurs

These reptiles were close relatives of the plesiosaurs. They had short necks and large heads and they were very fierce hunters.

Macroplata facts

Lived: 200 million years ago

Found: Europe

Length: 16 feet

Taking a breath

A pliosaur's nostrils were on the top of its head. This meant it could easily poke its head above the surface to breathe.

Macroplata

This early pliosaur had a long neck, like a plesiosaur. But unlike plesiosaurs, its rear flippers were larger than the front ones.

Peloneustes

Peloneustes had strong cone-shaped teeth. Its jaws were strong so it could bite and hold onto prey, such as large fish and squid and even plesiosaurs.

Peloneustes facts

Lived: 145 million years ago

Found: Asia, Europe

Length: 10 feet

Macroplata had a large, long head with rows of teeth like a crocodile.

Kronosaurus facts

Lived: 140 million years ago

Found: Australia

Length: 30 feet

Kronosaurus

This pliosaur was a fierce hunter. It had a huge head that measured nine feet long and a lot of big sharp teeth. It could move quickly by flapping its long flippers.

Ichthyosaurus

A lot of fossils of this reptile have been found so it is one of the best known of all prehistoric animals. This species lived for more than 60 million years.

Fossil food
Ichthyosaurus ate fish, squid, and curly shelled ammonites. Fossils of all these creatures have been found with ichthyosaur remains.

Big eyes for hunting
Skeletons show that ichthyosaurs had very big eyes. A species called *Ophthalmosaurus* had the largest. They were 4 inches across.

Super senses
Ichthyosaurus's big eyes helped it see in the darkness of the deep ocean. With its ears, it could also sense ripples in the water, made by moving prey.

Fine fossils
Some of the ichthyosaur fossils that have been found are in very good condition. They have many bones arranged next to each other as they would have been when the animal was alive.

Ichthyosaurus could crack an ammonite's hard shell with its strong jaws.

How deep?

We don't know how deep *Ichthyosaurus* could dive to find prey. Relatives of the type of squid it ate live in very deep oceans today, down to over 3,000 feet.

Eggs or babies?

Ichthyosaurus could not come to land to lay eggs. It gave birth to its young in the water, like dolphins do today.

Ichthyosaurus facts

Lived: 200 million years ago

Found: Europe, N. America

Length: 6 feet

Mosasaurus

This huge creature was a fierce hunter, even more powerful than the biggest sharks today. It could catch almost anything in the ocean, even giant turtles.

Origins

The ancestors of mosasaurs were probably big meat-eating lizards. These lizards began living in the ocean and their legs gradually became paddlelike flippers.

Feather-food

This early kind of bird, called *Hesperornis*, would have made a tasty snack for a mosasaur. The bird stood about as tall as a person. It could not fly, but it could paddle along with its big webbed feet.

What's in a name?

Mosasaurs are named after an area in the Netherlands called the Meuse. Their name means "Meuse lizards." Huge fossil jaws and teeth from a mosasaur were dug up there in the 1770s.

Swimming tail

This reptile's flippers were small and weak. It probably swam by moving its long body and tail from side to side like a huge snake.

When mosasaurs died out, sharks like this one took over the oceans.

Mosasaurus facts

Lived: 70 million years ago

Found: Europe, N. America

Length: 33 feet

Mosasaur skeleton

The skeleton of a mosasaur shows that it had arm and leg bones like a lizard. It also had a bendy lower jaw like monitor lizards of today.

Quick Quiz

Find the correct stickers to answer the questions below.

Which of these reptiles was one of the first plesiosaurs?

Answer

Cryptoclidus   Plesiosaurus   Muraneosaurus

Which of these pliosaurs had cone-shaped teeth?

Answer

Peloneustes   Macroplata   Kronosaurus

Which of these reptiles had very big eyes?

Answer

 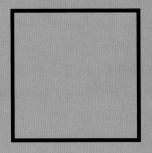

Ichthyosaurus   Elasmosaurus   Mosasaurus

Index

Index